Contents

The Sorrowful Mysteries

The Glorious Mysteries

Appendices: Varia Rosaria

To
My fellow Knights of Columbus

For
Their Love and Loyalty
To our Lord and our Lady
Through their Christian Life
And Regular Recitation of the
Holy Rosary

In memory of
Charlotte B. Smalley
who even in death
inspired this work

In gratitude to
Francese McTigue and daughter Kathy Boland,
who put their high-tech gadgetry
to use in the necessary communications
between author and editor,

and to
Sue Elliott,
who transcribed this writing and added
appropriate embellishments. Thanks also
to her husband, Guy, and her family, who
endured the ordeal in holy patience.

Letter to the Reader

Dear Reader,
Just a few observations:

One: The conceptual title of this book was *Beads in Motion*. This, of course, referred to the rosary beads slipping steadily through my fingers, as yours do, bead by bead, whether we sit or stand. This volume is the result of praying the rosary swaying at my side as I walk each day, reciting all twenty decades and meditating on what you'll find here recorded.

Two: I have quoted from the 1986 *New American Bible*, since I believe the average person will have that version in their home to which they may refer.

Three: My format, the indentations, is intended to slow down your reading, yes, so that you might let what I've written sink in a little deeper. My intent, too, is to leave you space to jot down in the margins your own reveries and inspired insights.

Four: This is the first of my planned four divisions into why, when, where, and who, which will afford you, I pray, fresh approaches to your rosarian meditations.

Five: There are fine videotapes available on the market depicting the rosarian mysteries and the prayers lcd by the holy father and others, including children. These are great for family and other groups. I recommend them as adjuncts to what I've written here.

Lastly: On October 16, 2002, the 25th anniversary of his election to the papacy, Pope John Paul II published his apostolic letter *Rosarium Virginis Marie*. In it he offered five new Mysteries of Light (also known as the Luminous Mysteries) to fill the void between the Joyful and Sorrowful Mysteries. They are a dream, a delight. See for yourself—I have included them in this volume.

Blessings! Be happy. Know you're loved.
Father Chester

The Joyful Mysteries

1. The Annunciation

2. The Visitation

3. The Nativity

4. The Presentation

5. The Finding of the Christ-Child in the Temple

The First Joyful Mystery

Why the Annunciation?

The Design Divine

From all eternity Father, Son, and Holy Spirit,
- foreseeing the fall of the human race
- through its misuse of that
- God-given gift of freedom (free will),
- planned to help the human family regain
- divine favor and friendship.

Since the offense was a sin against God,
- God himself would come to planet earth
- in the person of his Son.

He would live, love, suffer, and die for us.
Therefore, he would be truly human.
Hence, he would have a human mother.
That mother would be Mary.

Since she was to bear the sinless Son
- She too would be sinless
- made so by an extraordinary
    providence of God
- which would prevent
- even the slightest stain of sin
- ever to soil her
- or the power of the Evil One
- ever to master her.

The Plan in Action

So, when the "fullness of time" (Gal 4:4) had come:

> The angel Gabriel was sent from God
> to a town of Galilee called Nazareth,
> to a virgin betrothed to a man named Joseph,
> of the house of David, and the virgin's name
> was Mary (Lk 1:26–27).

The Message and the Messenger

Why an angel?
That's what an angel is for.
The word "angel" means "messenger."
Nothing else—no one else would do,
  · for so serious and solemn a moment in human history.

Mary is startled, of course.
We mere mortals experience a holy dread
  · in the presence of the supernatural.

Mary was no exception.
Hence, the first words from the angelic messenger:

> "Do not be afraid, Mary" (Lk 1:30).

Then, having allayed Mary's fears,
  · the angel greets this modest maiden
  · in a most gracious fashion:

> "Hail, favored one!
> The Lord is with you.
> … you have found favor with God" (Lk 1:28,30).

Mary is startled, puzzled
  · by so highly complimentary a greeting.

This, in an age when compliments,
  · especially compliments to a woman,
  · were few and far between.

But this greeting is more than a compliment.
This greeting embodies:
- the unique role and relationship
- Mary has to God
- and to the people of God
- as defined by the Trinity
- from all eternity.

The angel, then, delivers his core message:

> "You will conceive in your
> womb and bear a son" (Lk 1:31).

Then the immediate reaction
- from a woman recently married
- but not yet cohabiting
- with her husband,
- as was Mary:
  "I have no relations with a man?" (Lk 1:34).

The angel explains:

> "The holy Spirit will come
> upon you, and the power
> of the Most High will
> overshadow you. Therefore the
> child to be born
> will be called holy, the Son of God" (Lk 1:35).

Mary is astonished — overwhelmed, really.
First, she is told
- about the coming of the Messiah,
- something one would expect
- of the high-priest
- or a holy hermit or some prophet
- to be told.

And, that the Messiah
- will be God
- and she—his mother?

"How can this be?" Mary marvels.
"Who am I that I should be so highly
honored?" Mary muses.
  • In mod American, "Why me?"

But Mary is God's
  • good and faithful servant,
    first and always.

So, her humble reply,
  • one to echo down the ages:

> "Behold, I am the handmaid of the
> Lord. May it be done to me according
> to your word" (Lk 1:38).

At that moment, at Mary's famous "Fiat":
  • the Third Person began mystically
  • to form and fashion
  • the body of the Second Person
  • in Mary's immaculate womb.

And the redemption
    of the human race had begun.

The most singular and most significant event
  • on planet earth, more,
  • since the creation of the universe itself.

The Second Joyful Mystery

Why the Visitation?

More Good News

The final message to Mary from the angel:

> "Elizabeth, your relative,
> has also conceived a
> son in her old age, and this is the sixth month
> for her who was called barren;
> for nothing will be impossible for God" (Lk 1:36–37).

In effect, the first miracle, Mary's child,
- is being confirmed
- by a second miracle, Elizabeth's son.

Not that Mary required or requested
- such an attestation.

Reverie: I like to believe that this last info
- was given by the good Lord
- for all generations
- to see, hear and rejoice in, down the ages.

Kissing Cousins

Mary surely sank to her knees to make
- a profound act of thanksgiving
- for the graces heaped upon her
- so lavishly and so lovingly.

Then off she hurried
- to be of service and aid
- to her aged, expecting kin.

And the moment that Mary's greeting
- fell on Elizabeth's ear,
- Elizabeth, filled with the Holy Spirit,
- exclaimed with great joy and jubilation:

"Most blessed are you among
women, and blessed is
the fruit of your womb.
And how does this happen to me, that the
mother of my Lord should come
to me?" (Lk 1:42–43).

Now both women were wondrously aware
 • of the divine dimensions
 • to their maternity.

Mary, then broke out
 • into a magnificent paean (hymn) of praise:

"My soul proclaims the greatness of the Lord;
   my spirit rejoices in God my savior …
The Mighty One has done great things for me,
   and holy is his name" (Lk 1:46–47,49).

Reverie: How those two must have
 • laughed and cried,
 • prayed and sighed,
 • till Elizabeth delivered her child.

Then Mary had to go home.

What's happening there?

The Third Joyful Mystery

Why the Nativity?

Joseph's Dilemma and Dream

Joseph now is next to be informed
  • of his role in heaven's reasoning
  • for the redemption of the human race:

> "Joseph, son of David,
> do not be afraid to take
> Mary your wife into your home.
> For it is through the holy Spirit
> that this child has been
> conceived in her. She will bear
> a son and you are to name
> him Jesus, because he will
> save his people from their sins" (Mt 1:20–21).

Joseph, like Mary, is astounded.
Here he was, about to divorce Mary,
  • privately, of course,
  • having discovered her pregnant.

Now he's told Mary's offspring
  • is of divine origin
  • and he is being asked
  • to be the foster father
  • of the Messiah—God
  • and his rightful heir as well.

How can this be, muses Mary's husband.
But like his beautiful bride,
  • like his saintly spouse,
  • Joseph, too, is God's good and faithful servant.

Joseph accepts this awesome assignment
  • and this high honor humbly.

Six months later when he helps deliver the child
- he is also amazed
- at the magnitude of God's love
- for us sinful folk.

The Messiah, the awaited one, even before he's born
- has begun to suffer:
- "because there was no room for them in the inn" (Lk 2:7)
- on that first Christmas Eve.

And on that first Christmas night
- condescending to be born
- in a stable cave
- with the poorest of the poor
- as his first worshipers,
- the shepherds.

Reverie: Let's join these shepherds,
- kneel with them around the crib
- and adore Christ the Lord.

That's why he was born,
- to be loved, to be adored.

The Fourth Joyful Mystery

Why the Presentation?

Name Calling — The Right Way

At the age of eight days the child
- is given the name "Jesus"
- as directed by the angel Gabriel,
- a name identifying him
- with his sacred mission (Lk 2:21),
- "Yahweh saves," that is, "Savior."

Accompanying the name-giving
- was the ritual of circumcision
- as mandated by Mosaic Law.

Reverie: And so, at age eight days
- Jesus sheds his blood for the first time
- in our behalf, for our sake.

Why in our behalf?
Because, opting to be born a human being
- to become a member of God's chosen people, a Jew,
- he obligated himself to observe
- all the rituals, rules, traditions, customs
- of the Jewish faith.

Precious Baby, Precious Blood

One single drop of that precious baby's blood
- could have sufficed, there and then
- to redeem the human race.

But Father, Son, and Holy Spirit
- had other plans.

The Son would shed his blood again,
- and to the last drop at that,
- but not today, not till Good Friday.

God Is Offered to God

Then, at forty days of age
  · the child Jesus is taken to Jerusalem
  · by Mary and Joseph (cf. Lk 2:22).

Reverie: Oh how those infant eyes must have sparkled
  · as Jesus through those human eyes
  · saw for the first time
  · what as God he foreknew and foresaw
      from all eternity,
  · the resplendent Temple,
  · before, during, and after its completion
  · but now still under construction.

There, Jesus is presented to the Lord
  · since "dedicated," "belonging" to him,
  · as was every first-born Hebrew male (Ex 13:12);
  · then "redeemed" (released for secular pursuits) (Ex 13:13–15).
Mary, meanwhile, meekly submits
  · to a "purification ceremony"
  · even though she is the purest person
      on planet earth.

The Odd Couple?

Then there's this elderly man and woman
  · entering the Temple for the umpteenth time.

The Evangelist styles the man "righteous and devout" (Lk 2:25).
Most of all: "The holy Spirit was upon him" (Lk 2:25).
He yearns and pines
  · to see the "Anointed of the Lord"
  · the Messiah, the deliverer of Israel,
  · before he dies.

He is inspired by the Spirit of God
  · to enter the Temple,
  · to be in the right place at the right time.

He is given the grace
- to recognize the Messiah
- in the arms of this poor, humble
- but beautiful young mother
- standing alongside her husband, a village carpenter.

Simeon reaches out to Mary.
Without a moment's hesitation
- Mary places her precious baby gently
- into the ancient's eager, awaiting arms.
He looks with rapture on him
- for whom he had so long yearned and pined.

He raises his Redeemer heavenward
- and offers this, his humble prayer, the
  famous "Nunc Dimittis" (Canticle of Simeon):

> "Now, Master, you may let your servant go
> in peace, according to your word,
> for my eyes have seen your salvation,
> which you prepared in sight of all the peoples,
> a light for revelation to the Gentiles,
> the glory for your people Israel" (Lk 2:29–32).

Jesus' parents marvel at this moving performance.
Simeon then utters these sad prophetic words:

> "This child is destined for the fall and rise of many
> in Israel, and to be a sign that will be contradicted" (Lk 2:34).

In effect, the oldster is saying the mother would share
     in her Son's suffering.
Then another dire prediction
- directed personally at Mary:
  "and you yourself a sword will pierce" (Lk 2:35).

Reverie: This prophecy, that would reach its lowest depths
     on Good Friday,
  • had already begun on Christmas Eve
  • when Mary felt the sharp edge of that sword:
  • "No room" for him and her,
  • and on Christmas night,
  • no place, but no place
  • to lay the newborn Savior and God
  • except in a manger
  • of a stable-cave (Lk 2:7).

Besides Simeon there is present that other person, Anna.
She too has been yearning and pining
  • to see the Messiah before she dies.

A widow as well as a prophetess, in her eighties,
  • praying, fasting, found constantly in the Temple.

She too is given the grace to recognize
  • Mary's child as the "redemption of Jerusalem."
Then in her ecstasy and excitement,
  • if you'll pardon my own ecstasy and excitement,
  • she tells all who like her were awaiting the Savior
  • that her dream had come true at last.

Reverie: I can see her stopping people with her
  • joyous message:
  • "The Messiah has come;
  • he is here.
  • I know.
  • I've seen him with my own eyes."

The Fifth Joyful Mystery

Why the Finding of Christ in the Temple?

A Tough Assignment?

Every year the Holy Family
  - journeyed to Jerusalem
  - for the high-holidays, the Passover feast.

Reverie: Oh, how the boy Christ thrilled
  - to see and hear his heavenly Father
  - worshiped in so resplendent a manner.

And then being permitted when of age
  - to take active part in the divine services.

Time Out!

But when twelve, of puberty age,
  - the lad stays behind in the Temple
  - after the ceremonies are ended.

Meanwhile, Mary and Joseph
  - exit the building from different sides
  - since the sexes worshiped separately.

Each heads homeward in different groups
  - till the groups rejoin a little later
  - as was the custom.

It was then at their reunion
  - to their great, great grief and dismay
  - that they discovered their son missing.

Each had assumed he was in the other's company.
But the boy Christ was on a special assignment.
He had a mission to accomplish
  - in behalf of his heavenly Father.

And the Son is only twelve.

Jesus makes his way
  • to the priests' quarters.

There with those Temple priests
  • Jesus spends the next three days,
  • astounding them with the profundity
  • of the questions he puts to them
  • and by the brilliance
  • of his answers to the questions they put to him.

Reverie: The purpose I love to ascribe to myself
  • was to indicate to these priests
  • that the Messiah had already come
  • and that he would make himself known
      when of age.

A smile must have lit up the boy's face,
  • my imagination still at play,
  • for Jesus knew what they didn't know,
  • that he was the Messiah.

A Happy Ending

Arrive then Mary and Joseph,
  • astonished and amazed:

Mary: "Son, why have you done this to us? Your father
      and I have been looking for you
      with great anxiety."

Jesus: "Why were you looking for me? Did you not know
      that I must be in my Father's house?"
      (Lk 2:48,49; the entire Temple episode is in Lk 2:41–52).

Both questions are fraught with deep mystery.

Reverie: Can't you just picture what followed?
The Son that was lost, hugging, embracing
  • his tear-stained parents
  • till all three are smiling again.

Jesus then returns with Mary and Joseph to Nazareth
- to live the holiest and happiest home life ever lived,
- to grow in size and strength, physically,
- and spiritually in grace and wisdom
- before God and his fellow man (Lk 2:51–52).

The Mysteries of Light

1. The Baptism in the Jordan

2. The Wedding at Cana

3. The Proclamation of the Kingdom of God
   and the Call to Repentance

4. The Transfiguration

5. The Institution of the Eucharist

The First Mystery of Light

Why the Baptism in the Jordan?

The Baptized and His Baptizer

Jesus left Mary and home, Nazareth,
  • at about thirty years of age.

He had a mission
  • to be what he had been born to be,
  • the light of the world,
    and a message
  • to deliver to the world from his heavenly Father.

His first stop, the River Jordan.
There, John the Baptizer, son of Zechariah (Lk 3:2)
  • was exhorting great crowds
  • to repent of their sins
  • and, through his baptismal bath,
  • be cleansed of them (Lk 3:3).

Jesus approaches John as if he, Jesus,
  • were such a sinner.

Why?
Since when would the sinless Son of God
  • in human form need to be cleansed
  • of sins he had never committed?

John, too, under impulse and inspiration,
    • having pointed out the approaching Christ
    • "Behold, the Lamb of God, who takes
      away the sin of world" (Jn 1:29), demurs:

      "I need to be baptized by you,
        and yet you are coming to me?" (Mt 3:14).

John had reason to say this because
  • he had been saying all along:

"A man is coming after me
who ranks ahead of me
because he existed before me" (Jn 1:30).

Reverie: I like to picture Jesus gently squeezing John's arm,
• a faint smile gracing his holy face,
• then his determined, divine decision:

"Allow it now, for thus it is fitting
for us to fulfill all righteousness" (Mt 3:15).

I am in awe that these words are the adult Christ's
• first to be recorded in Scripture, shedding
• light on Jesus' double duty here,
• to allow John to baptize him
• and so fulfill his heavenly Father's will.

And why the Father's will that he, sinless,
• should be seen in a sinner's stance?

Because it was the divine intent that
• the Redeemer of mankind in flesh form
• should, as far as it was feasible,
• enter into the solidarity of sinful humanity,
• be one, or at least be seen, regarded,
• as truly of it.

The Son would prove his divine nature
• by his subsequent godly teaching and miracles
• and holiness of life and love for humanity.

Hence, Jesus, emerging from the peaceful, placid Jordan
• for all the assembled sinners
• to see and nod their approval,
• and to reckon him a reclaimed
• and cleansed sinner, as one of themselves,
• Jesus can now move on to his mission,
    his holy assignment.

He possesses, as it were, from John the Baptizer
• whom all there, and elsewhere, regarded
• as indeed a holy man, a prophet,
• an endorsement, a stamp of approval

and proved authenticity,
• worthy of credence and respect.

So, Jesus, thanks to this humbling of himself,
• identifying himself with his fellow humans
• can indeed begin to enlighten the world.

Thus, another John, John the Evangelist,
• in his profound prelude to his Gospel
• rightly observes:

> A man named John was sent from God.
> He came for testimony, to testify
> to the light, so that all might believe ...
> He was not the light ... but came to testify
> to the light (Jn 1:6–8).

Then the illuminating dazzling truth:

> The true light, which, enlightens
> everyone, was coming into the world (Jn 1:9).

Finally, what an exciting, endearing ending
• by the apostle whom Jesus loved:

> From his fullness
> we have all received, grace
> in place of grace (Jn 1:16).

As if this weren't enough
• we see a direct, divine sign of approval:

> After Jesus was baptized, he came
> up from the water and behold,
> the heavens were opened [for him],
> and he saw the Spirit
> of God descending like a dove [and] coming
> upon him. And a voice came from the
> heavens, saying, "This is my beloved Son,
> with whom I am well pleased" (Mt 3:16–17).

Isaiah was so accurate when he foretold:

> Upon those who dwelt in the land of gloom
> a light has shone (Is 9:1).

Reverie: Thomas Edison's invention, the electric light,
- puts an end to a dim past
- with its fitful, flickering torches, smelly kerosene
  lamps, dripping candles.

The light that Jesus brought illumines
- every nook and cranny of human existence,
- such as no other form of light
- could ever produce.

The Second Mystery of Light

Why the Self-Manifestation at Cana?

The Gracious Guest

Fresh from the waters of the Jordan
  • Jesus chooses his first followers,
  • forever known now as "The Twelve."

Then he and they receive an invitation to a wedding
  • at Cana in Galilee (Jn 2:1–2).

Reverie: I always wondered how this newly formed group
  • is suddenly included in the invite.

I suspect Mary had something to do with it
  • or because news had spread through
  • the small towns of Nazareth and nearby Cana
  • that the "local boy" is now preacher and teacher.

Hence, it was proper and polite to invite his new friends and followers.

My other opinion is that the Holy Family
  • was related or was a friend of the couple and
      their families;
  • thus the invitation would include
  • now Jesus' new extended family.

Of course, basically it was divine providence at work.
The eternal plan unfolding little by little
  • for the Light of the World to shine on.
Then Evangelist John, now also an invited guest,
  • tells us about an unexpected problem
  • occurring at the feasting and drinking at the
      wedding banquet.

The wine ran out (Jn 2:3).
And who noticed this?
Who else but someone who by her nature,
   • being the mother of Jesus,
   • therefore, the most caring creature in that crowd, no doubt:
      Mary.

Her observant eye and maternal instinct
   • foresaw what an embarrassment
   • would befall the newlyweds
   • were the most enjoyable part of their wedding
      feast to turn dry.

And to whom does Mary turn?
To the one who alone could do something—and fast.
Her divine Son, of course.
Her simple statement to him:
      "They have no wine" (Jn 2:3).

A surprising, cryptic reply to her:
      "My hour has not yet come" (Jn 2:4).

Jesus is saying his time-table
   • doesn't call for him to show his light … yet.

Is this a no?
Not for a single second.
Mary merely makes her way to the waiters
   • standing around, stunned by the unexpected
      and embarrassing situation.

They will be stunned even more as Mary instructs them:
      "Do whatever he tells you" (Jn 2:5).

In other words: Not to worry.

Reverie: I imagine Mary already knows a miracle is in the offing.
And what a miracle:

> Now there were six stone water jars
> there for Jewish ceremonial washings,
> each holding twenty to thirty gallons.
> "Fill the jars with water."
> So they filled them to the brim (Jn 2:6–7).

I also wondered what those waiters
- must have been thinking as they began refilling
  the jars,
- since the water by now was no longer needed for
  washing feet.

I also smile at the practical need to
- wash the feet of people entering a home.

It was more than a ceremony.
It was sheer necessity.
You see, people wore no shoes, only open sandals in those days.
And the streets were unpaved, filthy
- with animal and human waste,
- mud, dust, debris everywhere (litter-bugs even then).

Back to the waiters finishing their task;
- Jesus gives Mary a sideways glance;
- did he wink at her too?

Reverie: Not mentioned, but I love to imagine
- Jesus standing over all those jars
- containing more than one hundred gallons of fresh water.

Did he say a silent prayer?
Make the sign of the cross or extend his hands over them?
It was Richard Crashaw, Jesuit poet
- of English persecution times, if I remember rightly,
- who left us a very memorable, moving line about this scenario in a
  work entitled "Epigram":

> The conscious waters saw their
> God and blushed.

Terrific!

Reverie: I'm chuckling, fantasizing the surprise
- written on the waiters' faces
- as they see colorless water turn red.

I also smile at the thought of Mary,
- clapping her hands happily,
- running up to Jesus to hug him,
- whispering perhaps into his ear:

> "I knew you could, you would, do it, son.
> I'm so proud of you. Now the world will
> know what I always knew from Annunciation
> Day to Christmas. That you are God."

Jesus must have held her tightly too,
- rocking with her, eyes all aglow
- from that inner light that would illumine the world
  even more.

And the guests guzzling the wine, smacking their lips.
No cheap stuff here, for the waiter-in-charge,
- approaching the groom, observes:

> "Everyone serves good wine first,
> and then when people have drunk freely, an inferior one;
> but you have kept the good wine until now" (Jn 2:10).

John ends this exciting episode,
- this happy-ending event,
- this magnificent, miraculous occurrence:

> Jesus did this as the beginning of his signs
> in Cana in Galilee and so revealed his glory,
> and his disciples began to believe in him (Jn 2:11).

Right on!
Jesus' followers saw their Master's light
- and not only believed in him,
they followed him.

The Third Mystery of Light

Why the Proclamation of the Kingdom and Call to Conversion?

Hear Ye! Hear Ye!

Having turned on his holy light,
- focusing it on his divinity, his Godhead,
- as evidenced by the miracle at Cana,
- Jesus now proceeds to proclaim
- the kingdom of God to the public,
- to help all to see it clearer and sharper:

> "I have come to set the earth
> on fire, and how I wish it were
> already blazing!" (Lk 12:49).

That fire will be seen kindled, blazing bright
- in his first sermon, the Sermon on the Mount,
- as recorded by Evangelists Matthew and Luke (Mt 5:1–12; Lk 6:20–26)
- for all time.

It's on the eight Beatitudes,
- illuminating the darkened minds of his awed audience
- and setting their own hearts on fire.

His repeated, riveting word, "blessed,"
- the original wording, "happy,"
- eight times in Matthew, four in Luke (Lk 6:20–23),
- will be followed by a thrilling tribute
- to the followers themselves:

> "You are the light of the world …
> Just so, your light must
> shine before others, that they may
> see your good deeds and
> glorify your heavenly Father" (Mt 5:14,16).

Reverie: What a moving moment atop that blessed mount,
- mothers with their children wide-eyed
- at the immensity of the crowd and seeing
- the eyes of their own elders
- filled alternately with tears and the light of joy
- as the comforting words of the
- now solemn, now smiling speaker
- fills their ears with words and a
- message they had never heard before.

Teenagers suddenly silent and serious, for a change.
The aged somehow able to see and hear remarkably well.
It was, indeed, a blessed, happy moment.
The first of many more such words, providing
- comfort, consolation, and hope.

The Prayer of Prayers

It came in another setting, on another day
- not specified by the Scripture writers
- as to whether mountain, seashore, or desert,
- but on a topic of extreme importance,
- kept in the dark down the ages:
    The right relationship to God.
Hitherto, the pious Jew perceived the divine being
- as his creator, sustainer, liege lord,
- championing mightily, at times dramatically,
    his cause, his rights.

But mostly a force, a power,
- invisible, impersonal, untouchable,
- whose name, Yahweh, he was
- forbid to utter, even in prayer.

The Son of this Creator, this Lord, this fearsome force,
- tells this pious folk
- how to pray, how to perceive
- their God as he really is:
    A Father—a loving Father:

"This is how you are to pray:
'Our Father in heaven, … '" (Mt 6:9).

Jesus' kind of prayer chases away for all time
  · the shadows shrouding their impersonal deity.

Jesus, thus, turns the spotlight
  · not on the one who is omnipotent only
  · but on him who is truly a person,
  · a person they can identify with,
  · someone you can feel, touch, love.

Reverie: How I wish I were there that blessed moment,
  · to see those once dull eyes of
  · mothers and fathers suddenly brighten,
  · to watch mouths tightly closed
  · now gaping wide at the wonder of it all.
And the smiles, thousands of smiles,
  · on every man, woman, child, teenager, elder,
  · single, celibate, married, widowed.

People turning to one another to shake hands, to hug, to kiss.
Were it today, they'd let out cheers, hurrahs, applaud.
Today they'd stamp their feet, rise
  · and give Jesus a standing ovation.

And Jesus, Son of that same loving Father,
  · standing there, resplendent, radiant
  · against the setting sun
  · bowing slightly, right, left, center.
Is that a halo I see over his head?
Must be my imagination …

I, standing on the edge of the crowd on a slight rise,
  · give the Lord the thumbs-up sign.

He acknowledges with a soft smile.
His eyes, like his heart, are aglow.
They lift upward, heavenward.
To the Father.

The Undimming Light

Most of the light shed hitherto
  • was focused on Jesus' divinity.

His light was ethereal, unearthly, heavenly.
He himself was the "the true light ... coming into the world" (Jn 1:9).

The Rejected Light

But there would be some
  • who would not accept this light.

There were angry, hostile winds swirling,
  • attempting to extinguish this light.

And from where you would least expect,
  • from God's own sanctuary in Jerusalem,
  • the Temple.

From four sets of fierce foes fighting
  • this upstart, this innovator, this violator of the Law
  • claiming to be not only the Messiah
    but God himself.

These familiar but unfriendly forces belong
  • to the Pharisees, Scribes, Saducees, Herodians.

These unlikely opponents unite to oppose the Savior
  • on the basis of their own acquired prejudices.

How often the compassionate Christ
  • stopped, stooped, turned to, touched, lifted up
  • those pitiable, poor children of his Father,
  • needing help, seeking relief,
  • even though it was on the Sabbath.

And they, those Pharisees,
  • how insensitive to suffering humanity
  • crying out for help now, right now.

> But they: "No. Sorry. Not today.
> Come tomorrow.
> When it's lawful."

Jesus wouldn't stop, of course:

> "My Father is at work until now,
> so I am at work" (Jn 5:17).

It would cost him his life.

Guilt and the Guilty

Jesus' light would also fall on sin and forgiveness.
For instance, remember when this Redeemer
  • so appropriately, undauntingly dared
  • the assembled Scribes and Pharisees,
  • poised to stone to death
  • a woman caught in adultery,
  • to begin their gruesome execution
  • provided they themselves were free from sin.

Then his gentle question to the stricken, terrified, cowering woman,
  • after all had left, littering the area
  • with stones not thrown but dropped:

> "Has no one condemned you?"
> She replied, "No one, sir." Then Jesus
> said, "Neither do I condemn you" (Jn 8:10–11).

After the merciful absolution, then the quiet admonition:

> "Go, [and] from now on do not sin any more" (Jn 8:11).

What an inextinguishable light.
A light divine.

The Taxing Taxes

Even light was needed on the dark side of taxation
  • as it applied to both church and state.

The occasion?
When another clever trap was
  • laid by the Pharisees and Herodians (Mt 22:15–16),
  • each representing the religious and civic sectors
    of society.

The Lord is approached and confronted with this question,
  · which, no matter how answered,
  · would ensnare and incriminate him.

The question:

> "Is it lawful to pay the census tax [tribute]
> to Caesar or not?" (Mt 22:17; Mk 12:14; Lk 20:22).

Jesus asks to see a coin.
When shown the coin, Christ questions the lot:

> "Whose image is this and
> whose inscription?" (Mt 22:20; Mk 12:15; Lk 20:24).

The puzzled quizzers' reply:

> "Caesar's" (Mt 22:21; Mk 12:15; Lk 20:24).

The Redeemer's reply, still ringing down the centuries:

> "Then repay to Caesar what belongs
> to Caesar and to God what
> belongs to God" (Mt 22:21; Mk 12:16; Lk 20:25).

So much for clever traps.

Reverie: I think Christ kept a straight face
  · at the questioner's ensuing confusion and
     consternation.

But when alone later, in private with his own,
  · I can hear the Apostles roaring with laughter,
  · recalling the discomfiture and defeat
  · of their Master's most rabid opponents.

Jesus, I'm sure, wore a broad grin,
  · receiving congratulations modestly.

The boisterous shouts from all sides:

> "Wow! Wonderful work, oh wonderworker!
> You sure showed them up, boss.
> And they thought they had you by the throat!
> Great, Lord! Nice going!
> Hey, that was fun!"

We'd finish this section, glad that such a light
   • had been shed on so sizzling an issue as
   • taxation even with representation.

Social Studies

But there's still one more section to cover.
Jesus also has to proclaim the coming
   • of his Father's kingdom and
   • shed his light on some social issues.
So let's travel to another hot, hostile combat zone:
      Samaria.

Samaria is the home of the "renegade" Jews,
   • so styled, sad to say,
   • because half Gentile, half Jew.

The Samaritans—a break-away nation,
   • through no fault of their own,
   • a birth defect: one parent not kosher.

Only Well Water?

Jesus and his Twelve are passing through
   • Samaritan country one day (Jn 4:5–6).

They pause at a town called Shechem
   • where the Lord stops to rest at a nearby well.

The Twelve are sent shopping for groceries.
A woman comes to draw water (Jn 4:7).
Jesus asks for a drink.
She demurs it's improper for a Jew
   • to have any contact with Samaritans
   • even unlawful to address a woman,
   • any woman, in public,
   • except one's wife.

She's half-Jewish, remember.
Jesus' mysterious reply:

> "If you knew the gift of God and who
> is saying to you, 'Give me a drink,'
> you would have asked him
> and he would have given you living water" (Jn 4:10).

The words "living water" immediately
   • after her spirited defense of
   • the historic well and water where they are.
Jesus patiently explains:

> "Everyone who drinks this water will be thirsty again;
> but whoever drinks the water I shall give him will never
> thirst; the water I shall give will become in him
> a spring of water welling up to eternal life" (Jn 4:13–14).

The woman is enthralled, fascinated.
She begs this Jewish stranger to furnish her
   • with this wonder-water and its
      extraordinary powers.

Jesus, knowing this woman's past,
   • since he is also the all-knowing God,
   • tells her, kindly of course, to go home and fetch her husband.

She informs him she has no husband (Jn 4:16–18).
The Lord also knows this
   • and goes on to tell her, sadly, that she's had five husbands,
   • not counting the man she's living with now,
   • hence, not her husband.

The woman has pluck, though.
Give her credit because her reaction is positive:
      "Sir, I can see that you are a prophet" (Jn 4:19,25–26).

The upshot?
She hurries home, gently chastened, but reconciled,
   • announcing to all her neighbors
   • that there's a prophet in town,
   • maybe the long-awaited Messiah (Jn 4:28–30).

The townspeople come flocking to see.
They're convinced.
Jesus' light has shone again.
On acceptance, on tolerance, on the sanctity of marriage.
Voila!

The Fourth Mystery of Light

Why the Transfiguration?

Reverie: Everybody needs to take a breather,
  • today often a five-minute break.

All of us need the pause that refreshes
  • as a popular soda pop commercial put it.

There are time-outs, half-times,
  • seventh-inning stretches, etc., in sports.

Coaches and managers allow stoppage
  • when things get tough for their team.

So with Jesus.
His Twelve had traversed the Holy Land with him,
  • from Dan to Bersabe and back again,
  • had criss-crossed their country several times.

They were fatigued, tired of traveling on foot
  • the many miles their mission
  • and their Master's wishes deemed necessary.

They sensed his air of urgency in fulfilling his Father's will.
He had but three years to accomplish this.
He also knew his disciples were still assailed by doubts.
They needed a shot in the arm, a stimulus,
  • something different, something dynamic.

Jesus had just that in mind.

Mountain Grandeur

So, when in the neighborhood of a very high mountain,
  • traditionally thought to be Mount Tabor or Mount Hermon,
  • the Master let his group have their R and R, so to speak,
  • while he planned his next move.
Matthew narrates:

> After six days Jesus took Peter,
> James, and John his brother, and led them up
> a high mountain by themselves
> (Mt 17:1; see also Mk 9:2 and Lk 9:29).

Why these three?
We really don't know.
Jesus had good reasons, of course.
Very likely it was an in-house decision,
- Jesus knowing all his personally picked people,
- who met his specifications, so to speak,
- and these three had some certain
- talents and traits he needed.

Whatever the reasons, the Three represented all Twelve.
And there they were atop this mountain,
- with all its grandeur and greatness,
- with awe-inspiring views and vistas below.

But this was nothing compared to what followed:

> He was transfigured before
> them; his face shone like
> the sun and his clothes became
> white as light (Mt 17:2).

Reverie: Were you and I there, we'd drop
- to our knees, then prostrate ourselves,
- awed, overcome by this unexpected theophany.

My mind harkens back to the Old Testament.
In the desert the divine presence
- took the form of a column of a cloud by day
- and a column of fire by night,
- miraculous, marvelous, but material light.

Here we have the real, the real Jesus
- with his inner, divine light
- now shining through his physical physique.

Let Luke now tell us the next extraordinary event:

> And behold, two men were conversing
> with him, Moses and Elijah, who
> appeared in glory and spoke of his
> exodus that he was going to accomplish
> in Jerusalem (Lk 9:30–31).

Why Moses and Elijah?
These two are outstanding figures
- from Old Testament times:
- Moses, representing the Law;
- Elijah, representing the Prophets,
- the Law Jesus came to bring to perfection,
- the prophecies Jesus would fulfill.

They are heaven's emissaries
- discussing with Jesus his "passage,"
- meaning his death and return to life (resurrection).

I, too, stare in awe at them.
Were I sports fan, I'd run after them as they leave,
- hoping to get their autograph.

Now Peter, so overcome, so awed, so emotional
- and burning never to forget this transfiguration scenario,
- finally finds tongue
- but only to express a wild wish:

> "Master, it is good that we are here;
> let us make three tents,
> one for you, one for
> Moses, and one for Elijah" (Lk 9:33).

Reverie: Why tents? Like, say, circus tents?
Oh, now I remember. This magnificent
- self-manifestation of Jesus as God
- took place during the harvest festival
- when temporary shelters made of tree branches
- were set up to shelter guards watching out for
  would-be looters.

Or perhaps, a relic of ancient times when Israel
  · was surrounded by her enemies
  · and so had to secure the grain ready for harvest.

The shelters are called tents as well as booths (Hebrew: *succoth*).

The Father Speaks Again

Finally, the foremost and originally
  · the first witness to Jesus' divine origin, the Father:
  · the Father's voice is heard coming out of a
    luminous cloud:

> "This is my beloved Son,
> with whom I am well pleased;
> listen to him" (Mt 17:5).

Now it's the trio's turn to fall to the ground,
  · face down, in reverential fear (Mt 17:6).

The next thing they know, Jesus is standing over them;
  · touching them gently and speaking softly:
    "Rise, do not be afraid" (Mt 17:7).

Then the finale, a simple, single line:

> When the disciples raised their
> eyes, they saw no one else
> but Jesus alone (Mt 17:8).

The divine drama was over.
For now.
There would be a curtain-call.
But not till Easter.

The Fifth Mystery of Light

Why the Institution of the Eucharist?

A Divine Romance

Our Redeemer had many, many reasons to give us
- the most awesome and most
   mystery-laden sacrament
- of all the seven—the Eucharist.

All of these reasons are reducible to one:

Love

You see, God is love (1 Jn 4:7), eternal love.
And so, the Savior as the Son of God, therefore God,
- out of love for us gave us:

Life

Physical life, life of the body.
Then, to enhance this earthly life
- and preserve it for the life to come, eternal life,
- Jesus promised us, graciously, gloriously, divinely,
- this eternal, extraordinary existence
- on the occasion of feeding five thousand famished men,
- not counting women and children,
- gathered there to hear him, see him
- and be fed by him, physically.

Having fed them with earthly bread,
- he made the most outlandish promise
- in human history and memory:

> "I am the living bread that
> came down from heaven;
> whoever eats this bread will
> live forever; and the bread that I will give
> is my flesh for the life of the world" (Jn 6:51).

Some, stunned by this stupefying statement,
- never, but never, ever heard on this planet earth,
- found this too much,
- too much to understand, to accept.

The Lord hastened to say:

> "I say to you, unless you eat
> the flesh of the Son of Man and
> drink his blood, you do not have life
> within you. Whoever eats my flesh
> and drinks my blood has eternal life" (Jn 6:53–54).

Reverie: I'm convinced Jesus couldn't wait
- to keep this, his prodigious promise,
- and keep it he would.

On:

Holy Thursday Night

The night:
- celebrating his people's restoration to national life,
  life as a nation,
- at the Passover meal (the Seder supper),
- the Feast of the Unleavened Bread,
- the "Jewish Fourth of July."

Oh, how he poured out his heart before his followers that night:

> He said to them, "I have eagerly
> desired to eat this Passover with
> you before I suffer" (Lk 22:15).

What a spectacle, the most awesome scene
- since the creation of the world and the nativity
- for those gathered, for us for all time:

Then he took the bread, said
the blessing, broke it, and gave it
to them, saying, "This is my body
which will be given for you; do this in
memory of me." And likewise the
cup after they had eaten,
saying, "This cup is the new
covenant in my blood,
which will be shed for you" (Lk 22:19–20).

Reverie: Can't you just visualize the scene:
  · the apostles suddenly startled,
  · looking up wide-eyed, jaws dropping.

Huh?

Then the dawning on their minds.
The comprehension, followed by
  · the swift flashback to
  · the multiplication of the bread in the desert
  · with that puzzling promise
  · of the Eucharist, which, hey,
  · they now realize was being fulfilled before them.
"Oh, that's what he meant!
We had no idea how it could be,
  · how he could pull it off.
Glad we stuck with him anyway.
Those who left are gonna be sorry."

The Godhead's Hunger

What a brilliant, blazing light the Lord turned on!
A light on union, intimacy, oneness, closeness,
      with God.
How much closer could God get to us now
  · besides intellectual, emotional closeness?

Think about it.
Think food, in general:
- bread, meat, milk, snacks, pop,
- all these external, edible things
- are eaten by us
- and become us.

Food and drink turn into our eyes, ears, arms,
- the entire body,
- all that we are, physically.

This by a mysterious yet natural
- process called assimilation,
- bringing about a union, an integration
- that defies comparison with
- any other composite object.

Nailing, gluing, bonding, cementing, etc.,
- leaves the things to be brought together
- separate in themselves
- as close examination will show.

But there's nothing left of the food but the body it fed.

Reverie: What a God we have,
- so to yearn to be one with us.

How he loves us!
It blows the mind.
That yearning is now realized in the sacrament named:
  the Eucharist.

In it:
- we receive bread and wine,
- turned, transubstantiated into
- the Body and Blood of Christ,
- divine food and divine drink.

And do they become a part of us when we receive them?
No.
We become a part of Christ.
We become like Christ.
The giver becomes the gift.
And now we're one with God
  • in the closest possible union
  • that love could evolve, invent, so to speak.

Awesome.

But hey, wasn't God close to his
  • people Israel in the Old Testament?

A people he loved so much, cherished so dearly and deeply,
  • saved, liberated, guided, guarded so jealously.

He sure was close to them—
very close.
But the nearest thing to closeness
  • between God and his chosen people
  • the Old Testament could provide was
  • not yet ready for the kind of
  • love-union the Eucharist
  • in the New Testament, our times, has providentially provided.

The analogy, the closest comparison before Christ was the
  • union of husband and wife
  • two in one flesh,
  • marital intimacy, conjugal closeness.

Thus, for instance, Jeremiah is recorded saying, in effect:
  • the Lord is a husband (Jer 3:20),
  • a loving husband to
  • a wife, the people of God, Israel.

Especially, and more so
  • when the wife proved unfaithful
  • as often happened through Israel's long history.

Yet this divine spouse never broke their marriage bond.

Reverie: We Catholics for years called the Eucharist
  • "holy communion," a holy union.

Eucharist, a Greek word meaning "to give thanks,"
  • refers to Christ thanking his Father
  • when taking the bread and wine
  • before pronouncing the words of institution.

Both terms are relevant and reverend.
The reality is what counts.

The Priestly Role

That all his faithful would be
  • nourished and safeguarded
  • for eternal life through this sacramental food,
  • Christ, the eternal high priest that he is,
  • assigned the act of consecrating and serving
  • this sacramental food and drink
  • to the select group that gathered around him
  • on that unforgettable Holy Thursday night:

> "Do this in memory of me" (Lk 22:19).

Thus the "Last Supper Room," the upper room
(Mk 14:15; Lk 22:12), the Cenacle,
  • would convert into small chapels and splendid cathedrals
  • down the centuries and in every clime.

The wooden table before which the
  • eternal priest, Christ,
  • ordained his first priests
  • would become brother-altar to
  • those not only of wood but of marble as well
  • in sanctuaries reaching around planet earth,
  • as the prophet Malachi is understood to proclaim:

> For from the rising of the sun, even to its setting,
> my name is great among the nations;
> And everywhere they bring sacrifice
> to my name,
> and a pure offering (Mal 1:11).

Reverie: What a brilliant, blazing light
- on the priesthood and
- on the sacrifice of the Mass,
- the Holy Eucharist.

Yet, it's not always glamorous
- with colorful processions,
- fragrant incense,
- varied hued vestments,
- vast crowds, huge turn-outs,
- organs pealing, choirs chanting.

As a parish priest, hospital and
- quasi-military chaplain,
- I can't help but recall ruefully
- offering the Eucharist in less dramatic settings:

On a dining room table in the
- homes of sick, shut-ins, and dying parishioners.

On a swinging metal table alongside a hospital bed.

Once, under the spreading wings
- of a B-52 bomber, but in peace-time, thank God.

Even on a stump of a tree in a forest of Douglas firs
- where youthful cadets had hurriedly encamped.

Christ the light was visible there,
- in every setting, situation, circumstance,
- illuminating, brightening, bringing cheer,
  radiating love.

The Conclusion — But Not the End

These, then, are some of the highlights
- why Jesus instituted the Eucharist.

The most dazzling light of all:
The giver has given himself as a gift
- Who at the holy altar
- places himself sacramentally into
- the hands of a mortal priest,
- who in turn places him
- in your outstretched hand
- for immortality.

The Sorrowful Mysteries

1. The Agony in the Garden

2. The Scourging

3. The Crowning with Thorns

4. The Carrying of the Cross

5. The Crucifixion

The First Sorrowful Mystery

Why the Agony in the Garden?

A Dark Night — Yet a Night Divine

Twenty plus years have elapsed
- since the Temple episode
- when Jesus was twelve.

Tonight he's at Gethsemane, the Garden of Olives.
Gone now those happy, holy days at home.
Gone too those three astounding years
- of public life
- when he began to redeem the human race
- with his teaching, preaching, loving, forgiving.

He is alone.
Yet a little earlier at the paschal meal
- he had ordained the Apostles his first priests
- and given them their first Eucharist.

Where are they now?
Just a stone's throw away, sound asleep,
- too tired to watch and pray
- with their Master for even an hour (Mt 26:36–40).

And on his way to betray his Master is Judas,
- a participant at that first Eucharist.

The traitor is leading an armed rabble
- to seize his own Master
- and hand him over
- to those who rejected his Master's
- new way of life and love,
- works and words
- that were truly divine in origin and character.

And tomorrow:
- Good Friday, the bloody martyrdom.

So intense is the Lord's agonizing
- over these three tragic events
- that drops not of perspiration but of blood
- form on the Savior's sacred forehead.

The human Christ cries out from the depths
of his soul:

"My Father, if it is possible,
let this cup pass from me" (Mt 26:39).

The Father faithfully responds.
He sends an angel to strengthen his Son.
And the Son is strengthened
- for now the Son responds:

"Not my will but yours
be done" (Lk 22:42).

Jesus himself had taught us to say:
"Our Father ... your will be done" (Mt 6:9–10).

Jesus practiced what he preached.

The Second Sorrowful Mystery

Why the Scourging?

The Dirty Pieces of Silver

Judas now makes his appearance.
He left the Last Supper
  • as soon as he learned
  • that the Lord would be at Gethsemane.

In his pockets jingle the silver coins,
  • the first part of his dirty deal
  • with the high priests
  • and their foul followers.

The second part of this sinful scheme:
  • identifying the Master
  • in the darkness of the unlit garden
  • lest one of the Apostles
  • be mistakenly fingered.

Judas, however, is not alone.
He's accompanied by armed guards,
    Roman and Jewish (Jn 18:12).
Now the horrific moment,
  • the pre-arranged signal,
  • the traitor's hypocritical greeting:
    "Hail, Rabbi!" (Mt 26:49).

Followed then a kiss, blistering the Lord's lips.
And the suffocating embrace.
The nerve of the man.
Jesus, ever gentle, ever gracious, responds:
    "Friend" (Mt 26:50).

No recriminations.
No vituperations.
Just a quiet resignation from the Redeemer:
  "Do what you have come for" (Mt 26:50).

Meaning: I know what you're up to. Get it over with.

Reverie: Judas could have, should have,
  • fallen to his knees there and then
  • and made his first confession.

The Lord would have forgiven him.
Jesus loved Judas.
Jesus hand-picked him as an Apostle.
Just two words,
  • like "I'm sorry" or "Forgive me"
  • would have sufficed.

But later the enormity of his sin
  • overwhelms the unfortunate man.

Mistakenly he thinks he can't be forgiven.
Guilt-ridden, the betrayer turns away
  • from the one who loved him most.

He stumbles into the darkness
  • and there somewhere in that darkness,
  • or later the next day,
  • Judas takes his own life.

So deep is his despair.
How tragic!

The Phantom Hand

Meanwhile, Jesus faces the armed mob
  • as if to give it second thoughts
  • about its coming out against him
  • as if he were some criminal.

Christ calmly asks:
  "Whom are you looking for?" (Jn 18:4)

The answer:
> "Jesus the Nazorean" (Jn 18:5).

Jesus' reply:
> "I AM" (Jn 18:6).

Three times the question is asked
- and three times it's answered.

Each time the mob falls back
- as if struck by an invisible hand.

Then Peter (as identified by St. John; Jn 18:10)
- unsheathes his unauthorized sword,
- swings wildly and happens to strike
- of all people, the High Priest's servant,
  Malchus,
- severing the man's right ear (Jn 18:10).

Jesus at once raises his hand
- not to fell an injured enemy
- but to heal him.

The Master then rebukes Peter:

> "Put your sword back ...
> for all who take the sword will
> perish by the sword" (Mt 26:52).

Then in gentler tones:

> "Do you think that I cannot call
> upon my Father and he will not
> provide me at this moment
> with more than twelve legions
> of angels?" (Mt 26:53).

And the final words of holy resignation:

> "Shall I not to drink the cup
> that the Father gave me?" (Jn 18:11).

With that, and without any further violence,
- the Lord allows the mob to lead him away.

He is taken to the high priests,
- Annas and Caiphas,
- and there before them
- for the rest of the night
- he is verbally and physically abused
- and on the morrow, early,
- arraigned before Pontius Pilate,
- procurator (governor) of Judea.

The Stinging Scourges

Pilate addresses Jesus, demanding:
> "Are you the King of the Jews?" (Jn 18:33).

Comes Christ's calm reply:

> "Do you say this on your own
> or have others told you about me?
> ... My kingdom does not belong
> to this world" (Jn 18:34–36).

There and then Pilate should have
- dismissed the case;
- no evidence of any violation of Roman law here,
- no proof that a crime had been committed.

But, eventually after several futile feints
- the Governor fearing a riot
- and to appease the accusers
- sacrifices the accused (Jn 19:16).

The procurator orders his prisoner scourged.

Reverie: And so the Savior
- suffers those savage scourges
- to lacerate and bloody
- his sacred body
- as he atones for our sins
- committed by our bodies.

Famed artist Edward Manet painted
- a remarkable replica in oil of the scourging,
- entitling it *The Mockery of Jesus.*

The painting presents three different figures
  • surrounding the scourged Christ.

One is that of a brutal soldier gloating
  • over the effects of his evil work.

He's behind and to the left of the prisoner.
Kneeling at Jesus' feet is an ordinary layman
  • with agony is his eyes.

A third person, a raconteur, behind but to the right,
  • is peering down at the recumbent figure of Christ
  • with a questioning, puzzled look that asks:
    "Why?"

The Third Sorrowful Mystery

Why the Crowning with Thorns?

Hurt Heaped upon Hurt

As if the scourging weren't enough
- the soldiers devise a
- new and fiendish form
- of torture for their victim,
- a crown of thorns.

Earlier the soldiery were either present or heard about
- the prisoner being interrogated by Pilate
- as to whether the prisoner was a king.

Perhaps they forgot or didn't hear
- Christ's clear-cut answer:

> "My kingdom does not
> belong to this world" (Jn 18:36).

So, now Jesus suffers
- for our sins of thought
- and for the second time
- in less than twenty-four hours
- Jesus' sacred brow
- is bathed in blood.

Reverie: The needle-sharp thorns
- had done their utmost.

But Jesus is still our king
- whether his crown is of thorns
- or of gold.

Pontius Pilate now parades his prisoner
- before the mob.

He shouts at the ribald, jeering rabble:
> "Ecce Homo"
> ("Behold, the man!") (Jn 19:5).

If the governor expected pity and compassion
- to be shown to this,
- the most innocent of his prisoners
- yet the one most brutally beaten,
- he was badly mistaken.

He is showered with cat-calls and cries:
"Crucify him, crucify him!" (Jn 19:6).

The Unjust Judge

But fearing this time
- that he might be reported to Rome
- for releasing someone claiming
- to be a king, a rival of Caesar,
- hence a capital offense,
- Pilate calls for a basin of water,
- and coward that he is, shouts:

"I am innocent of this man's blood.
Look to it yourselves" (Mt 27:24).

He then hands Jesus over to be crucified.

In effect, this highest Roman official
- declares himself innocent,
- the prisoner also innocent,
- so go ahead, crucify him.

Finally Pilate washes his hands.

Reverie: Yet all the water in the world
- would not suffice
- to wash away the Savior's blood
- from Pilate's hands
- nor from the hands of those
- who also were responsible
- for this dark deed.

Then his swift legal query:

"Do you want me to release to you
the king of the Jews?" (Mk 15:9).

The mob, especially the conspirators and their ilk,
- as swiftly yell back:
    "We have no king but Caesar" (Jn 19:15).

Reverie: Pilate must have shaken his head in
    disgust and dismay
- especially at the irony of the last outcry:
    "We have no king but Caesar."

Pilate knew very well that no one hated Caesar
- more than these Jews.

And at this moment
- no one hated this Jesus more than
- this small band of mean-minded men
- who always wanted
- the prisoner dead.

The Fourth Sorrowful Mystery

Why the Carrying of the Cross?

The Bloody Footsteps

Jesus accepts this unjust sentence of death,
- the most heinous miscarriage of justice
- in human history.

Perhaps Jesus even embraced the cross
- as it had now become
- the instrument of our redemption.

Christ Jesus begins to carry the cross.
But now he is exhausted
- from a long night of torture and torment,
- from lack of food and rest,
- from loss of blood.

He begins to stumble.
He falters.
He falls.

Reverie: We pause here to ponder
- how we must help others carry their cross
- and lighten Jesus' load, the weight of our sins,
- by our good, Christian, moral life.

The Fifth Sorrowful Mystery

Why the Death on the Cross?

The Ascent to Glory

Jesus now reaches Golgotha, Calvary.
His cross now becomes an altar.
Three years earlier
- John the Baptizer pointed out Jesus
- to the immense crowds:

> "Behold, the Lamb of God,
> who takes away the sin of the world" (Jn 1:29).

Reverie: Jesus is indeed the Lamb of God,
- the perfect sacrifice.

For there on Calvary
- God is being offered to God;
- God the Son is offering himself
- to God the Father
- to atone for our sins,
- to redeem us
- out of love for us.

Nothing could be better than this.
Jesus is also the perfect offering
- because as a human being
- he can and does suffer
- to the utmost
- and as God, his suffering and death
- are of infinite, redemptive value.

The Tre Ore

Follow then the Lord's
- last will and testament,
- the fundamental answers
- to the "why?" for the crucifixion.

The seven last utterances:

1. "My God, my God, why have you forsaken me?"
    (Mt 27:46; Mk 15:34).
Jesus is quoting Psalm 22:1 here.
Jesus embodies the "righteous sufferer"
   • of that Psalm 22
   • who turns out to be
   • this crucified Christ.

Jesus did not wait nor expect
   • an answer to his excruciating cry.

Jesus was expressing his pain
   • as a human being.

His human nature
   • was experiencing extreme trauma.

His human body
   • was undergoing indescribable agony.

Jesus was expressing his pain
   • not in isolation
   • but in the aggregate,
   • with all his fellow humans
   • when they too would cry out
   • in their seeming isolation, loneliness,
   • yet never denying the divine presence.

Jesus in that most awful moment
   • still knew he was divine,
   • that glory was awaiting him,
   • as it awaits all who make
   • their agony redemptive, salvific,
   • and eventually, like Christ's, glorious.

2. "Father, forgive them, they know not what they do"
    (Lk 23:34).

Why forgive them?
Because they needed forgiveness.
Because it's the nature of God
   • to forgive.

To forgive is divine.
Forgiveness implies love.
And God is love.

3. "I say to you, today you will be with me in Paradise" (Lk 23:43).

Why forgive a criminal?

Because the criminal requested forgiveness.

> "Jesus, remember me when
> you come into your kingdom" (Lk 23:42).

Instant forgiveness.
The criminal was forgiven because he confessed
  • publicly at last,
  • acknowledging to his fellow criminal:

> "We have been condemned [to death] justly,
> for the sentence we received corresponds to
> our crimes, but this man
> has done nothing criminal" (Lk 23:41).

And the instant promise of a reward:

> "Amen, I say to you, today you will
> be with me in Paradise" (Lk 23:43).

The "thief" stole paradise,
  • sliding into home plate safely.

4. "Father, into your hands I commend my spirit" (Lk 23:46).

Why? Didn't the Father know his Son was dying?
Answer: The Son was expressing
  • his trust in his Father
  • to the very last.

Jesus was his Father's Son,
  • as from all eternity
  • so now, in his final moment
  • on earth
  • in his humanity.

To leave us a similar memory
- and wording
- when we are dying.

5a. "Woman, behold, your son" (Jn 19:26).

Why someone else's son, namely, John?
Because Mary had no other sons or daughters.
In turn, John will never forget Jesus telling him:

5b. "Behold, your mother" (Jn 19:27).

Why John, then, instead of another Apostle?
Because John was the one the Lord
- loved most,
- trusted most,
- stayed by the cross longer than most,
- never doubted his Master's divinity.

6. "I thirst" (Mk 15:23).

A physical thirst—under a broiling Asian sun.
A spiritual thirst—for your love and mine,
- for earlier, when teaching, Jesus said:

> "Whoever believes in me will
> never thirst" (Jn 6:35).

Yet, when offered the drink, the Lord
- refused it,
- so as to suffer for us to the utmost,
- so much did he love us,
- so great was his spiritual thirst
- for our reciprocated love.

Reverie: It's a sobering thought
- not only for those addicted to deadly alcohol
- but also for those who especially
- order and carry around large sixteen-ounce soft drinks,
- oversized, unnecessary, as also
- highly caffeinated espressos,
- with no thought or intent
- to mortify one's self,
- to atone for one's excesses,
- to feel a little what Jesus felt
- a lot.

7. "It is finished" (Jn 19:30).

Why now?
In effect it's the Father
- who is saying:

> "That's enough—
> My son has suffered enough."

And the son stating in kind:

> "I've done what you wanted, Dad.
> I did it just like you said I should."

Jesus is reporting to all of us:

> "You're saved.
> You are no longer dead in sin.
> My job is done."

And Jesus breathes his last.
Jesus dies.
But we live.

Retrospect

After three hours of the most
- agonizing, excruciating pain
- the Son and Savior
- surrenders his Spirit
- into his Father's hands.

Earlier Jesus stated:

> "I lay down my life
> in order to take it up again.
> No one takes it from me,
> but I lay it down on my own" (Jn 10:17–18).

Reverie: No power on earth, no physical force
- could separate the Lord's soul from his body.
- Only he could do that.
- And Jesus opts to do just that.
- Of his own volition
- he wills to die.
- He dies.
- But we live.
- Our salvation has been achieved.
- Our sins have been washed away.
- Thank you, Jesus. Thank you.

The Awesome Aftermath

All nature is convulsed in grief.
St. Matthew vividly paints the devastation:

> The earth quaked, rocks were split, tombs
> were opened, and the bodies of many saints
> who had fallen asleep were raised (Mt 27:51–52).

St. Luke adds:

> Darkness came over the whole
> land until three in the afternoon
> because of an eclipse of the sun (Lk 23:44–45).

Why all this?
It was nature's way, so to speak,
- of reacting in her grief
- to the death of her God in human form.

The sacred of Israel also reacts:

> The veil of the sanctuary was
> torn in two from top to bottom (Mt 27:51).

Scholars see the symbolism here:
  • the Old Testament is finished.

Pagan Rome too reacts
  • and favorably, surprising to say:

> The centurion, who stood guard over him,
> seeing the manner of his death, declared,
> "Truly, this was the Son of God!" (Mt 27:54).

Racing the Sun

Since the next day would be the Sabbath
  • Jewish custom called for
  • the removal of corpses from the cross
  • which required Pilate's permission.

Pontius Pilate is surprised, as those crucified
  • often agonized two to three days.

He authorizes their removal.
Another atrocious and barbaric procedure:
  • to insure death
  • legs of the crucified
  • were smashed by club-wielding soldiers.

The shock and severe injuries brought immediate death.
Seeing Jesus already dead,
  • one of the soldiers,
  • probably the officer in charge,
  • thrust a lance into the Lord's side.

Out flowed blood and water,
  • "the fountain of sacramental life
  • in the Church"
  • we hear sung in the preface
  • of the Mass of the Sacred Heart.

Joseph of Nazareth attended to the
  • details of Jesus' birth.

Now Joseph of Arimathea attends to the
- details of Jesus' burial,
- petitioning Pilate to release the body,
- supplying the shroud
- now believed the one in Turin.

Nicodemus, who came once to Jesus by night to learn,
- now comes as Jesus' undertaker,
- bringing the embalming ingredients:
- a mixture of myrrh and aloes
- weighing a hundred pounds.

The two sadly and probably teary-eyed
- bind the sacred body in wrappings
- reminiscent of Egyptian mummies.

There's a newly hewn tomb nearby,
- belonging to the Arimathean,
- in which no one had been laid.

Jesus is laid tenderly in it.
The sun is beginning to sink in the west.
Quickly the two head for home.
They reach it just in time.

Good Friday is no more.

The Sabbath stillness settles over
      the land.

The Glorious Mysteries

1. The Resurrection

2. The Ascension

3. The Descent of the Holy Spirit

4. The Assumption of Mary

5. The Coronation of Mary

The First Glorious Mystery

Why the Resurrection?

Homecoming Number One

From Calvary, Jesus' Spirit soars to eternity.
There an immense multitude of the dead
- is awaiting him, namely:
- all from Adam and Eve down,
- the faithful, the saints, the converted sinners,
- everyone expecting him to escort them
- into the immediate presence of the Father.

They're in heaven, but not yet in possession
- of the Beatific Vision,
- that is, seeing God face to face.

This, the most cherished of God's gifts to us
- was lost when the human race fell from grace.

The Redeemer, now the atoner of that fall,
- comforts this vast assemblage
- with the message
- that in forty-three more earth days
- he will do just that,
- lead them into his Father's
- immediate presence.

Then Jesus returns to earth.
In spirit he enters the tomb
- where lies his cold, lifeless body.
Body and soul of the Redeemer
- are reunited.

Jesus stirs into life.
He arises,
- triumphant, transfigured, glorious.

Reverie: I just can't help but picture the following scenarios:

The angels bow and salute the risen Son
- on his way, first, to be with the
- one he loved most and the
- one who loved him most,
- Mary.

Jesus: "Mother, I'm home."
Mary: "Oh son, Oh son, I knew you'd come back."

These first precious moments,
- are not recorded in Scripture
- as they are too personal, too intimate,
- as were the first years
- of Jesus' home-life,
- the hidden years of his
- childhood, boyhood, young manhood.

The theological reasons for the resurrection, however,
are infinite.

St. Paul sums them up:

> If Christ has not been raised,
> your faith is vain (1 Cor 15:17).

and:

> For since death came through a human
> being, the resurrection of the
> dead came also through a human being
> [Jesus] (1 Cor 15:21).

Reverie: We have an eternity to review
- all the other reasons.

The Second Glorious Mystery

Why the Ascension?

Ladies First

From Mary's side, the Son
  • returns to the tomb area.

This time to comfort
  • another Mary, Mary of Magdala.

She is at this moment
  • peering into the tomb
  • through the low, outer opening
  • from which the angel had
  • earlier rolled back a huge rock.

Her eyes are suffused with tears.
She mistakes Christ for the caretaker:
Mary: "Sir, if you carried him away, tell me
      where you laid him, and I will take him" (Jn 20:15).

Jesus: "Mary!" (Jn 20:16).

The Emmaus Road

Later that day, two of the Lord's disciples
  • also fail to recognize their Master
  • as he joins them on the road leading to Emmaus (Lk 24:13–35).

Not till evening at table
  • at the breaking of the bread
  • are their eyes opened.

Then the Savior vanishes from their sight.

The Last Supper Room Revisited

Hastily arising from their meal,
    · the two hurry back to the city
    · where the other disciples are gathered.

They recount their extraordinary experience,
    · how they didn't recognize the Master:

"Can you imagine our not recognizing him
    · till he blessed, broke, and distributed the bread to us
    · as he did at the Last Supper?

And, oh how our hearts," they recollected,
    · "burned within us on the road
    · as he explained to us
    · the Scriptures that pertained to his
    · suffering, death, and resurrection."

A little later the Lord appears in that same cenacle,
    · passing through the locked doors:

> "Peace be with you.
> As the Father has sent me,
> so I send you …
> Receive the Holy Spirit.
> Whose sins you forgive are forgiven them,
> and whose sins you retain are retained" (Jn 20:21–23).

The Doubter

At first, frightened and alarmed,
    · the Apostles are now ecstatic, overjoyed.

All now are convinced of the Lord's miraculous return
    · except Thomas who arrives late,
    · after the Lord had left.
Doubting more, disbelieving Thomas stubbornly insists:

> "Unless I see the mark of the nails
> in his hands and put my finger into the nailmarks
> and put my hand into his side, I will not believe" (Jn 20:25).

A week later, in the same cenacle,
  • Jesus reappears addressing Thomas, present this time:

> "Put your finger here and see my hands,
> and bring your hand and put it into my side,
> and do not be unbelieving, but believe" (Jn 20:27).

Thomas's shamed but sincere retraction:
  "My Lord and my God!" (Jn 20:28).

The Lord's forgiveness and follow through:

> "Have you come to believe because
> you have seen me?
> Blessed are those who have not seen
> and have believed" (Jn 20:29).

Fishing for Simon Peter

Later still, at the seashore, the gentle Jesus asks:

> "Simon, son of John, do you
> love me more than these?" (Jn 21:15).

Peter's agonizing but relieved reply:

> "Yes, Lord, you know that I love you" (Jn 21:15).

The question is tripled, all tolled,
  • as is the pardon:

> "Feed my lambs. …
> Tend my sheep. …
> Feed my sheep" (Jn 21:15–17).

Homecoming Number Two

Reverie: Then the final farewell by the Lord
  • to his faithful followers and friends
  • and especially to Mary.

His tender, touching, but nowhere recorded words:

> "I must leave now, mother dearest.
> But you're needed here.
> The church needs you."

Can't you just picture Mary responding
- wistfully but resignedly:
  > "I will miss you so, son."

Then the Lord Jesus ascends on high
- gloriously, majestically, moving up, up, up.

What a heavenly homecoming awaits him.
What a remarkable reunion:
- Father and Son together at last.

And as the angelic choirs
- chant the Son's praises,
- the Father crowns the Son
- for his heroic life, death, suffering here below,
- for redeeming the human race,
- for carrying out the Father's will in every detail.

Hail King Jesus.

Hail.

The Third Glorious Mystery

Why the Descent of the Holy Spirit?

A Ghostly Encounter

Mary was indeed needed with Jesus gone.
She was now the mother of the infant church.
And so her son's disciples gather around her
- as the first novena
- in the history of the church begins.

A novena to the Holy Spirit.
Prior to his ascension, Jesus instructed his adherents
- not to leave Jerusalem:

> "Wait for the promise
> of the Father about which
> you have heard me speak; … in a
> few days you will be baptized with
> the holy Spirit" (Acts 1:4–5).

Followed then nine days of intense prayers,
- prayers to the Third Person of the Trinity.

On the tenth day after Jesus' ascension
- the Holy Spirit arrives as promised.

He comes amid a mighty wind
- in the form of parted tongues
- as if of fire.

God has returned to his church.
We are now temples of the Holy Spirit.
The Third Person takes over.
The invisible God now leads
- the very visible people of God.

A Ship Launching

The Spirit descended, not in stillness under a starry sky
- as did the Son on Christmas night (Lk 2:8).

The Spirit made a dramatic entry to earth
- in broad daylight, for all to see and hear,
- amid a driving wind (Acts 2:1–2),
- the Third Person's own triumphant tempest.

Reverie: Why a mighty wind, this tempest?
- It's as if to billow out the sails of the
   good ship "Mother Church,"
- also known as, "Peter's Barque."

She weighs anchor after three and thirty years
- in the home port of her making, Israel,
- to drop anchor now in every port of the seven seas
- till dropping it for the last time
- when reaching her final destination
- in the eternal port called "Paradise."

Pentecostal Pyrotechnics

The Spirit also comes in fiery form (Acts 2:3):
- to enflame hearts with greater love
- than ever before, for God and man.

Fiery tongues—eloquence—gift of languages
- to set people on fire
- with zeal and burning desire
- to spread the truth
- of the good news, the Gospel truth,
- in every age and place
- till the end of time.

What a day!
Pentecost day.

The Fourth Glorious Mystery

Why the Assumption of Mary?

My Fair Lady

Reverie: Mary continued to be the focal point
  • of the church's prayer life,
  • that is, the church's private prayer life,
  • with friends and visiting folk.

What an inspiring sight also
  • at the church's public prayer life,
  • the celebration of the sacred liturgy.

Imagine Mary receiving the Eucharist
  • from the hands of the Apostles,
  • ordained for that most pious purpose
  • by her own son, Christ, eternal high priest.

Mary receiving her son once again
  • into her immaculate, inner self
  • but this time, sacramentally.

Then when her life's work was over,
  • the final farewells to all,
  • especially to the Apostle John.
Standing off to the side we picture hearing her say:

> "Thank you dear, dear John
> for taking such good care of me."

Then in her own reverie, as it were:

> "Even now I can see my Jesus
> saying to me from the cross,
> 'Woman, behold, your son'" (Jn 19:26).

It isn't difficult to imagine John replying in kind:

> "And how can I ever forget Jesus
> saying to me from the cross:
> 'Behold, your mother'" (Jn 19:27).

Then the outpouring of the Apostle's heart:

> "Oh, dearest Mother Mary,
> What a joy and a privilege it
> was to look after you, to take
> Jesus' place, unworthy though I am."

Finally the exquisite appeal:

> "Say hello to Jesus for me
> when you see him."

With that the Father leans down to earth
  • from his heavenly heights
  • and draws Mary's sweet breath unto himself.

And Mary dies.
She dies the most beatific, ecstatic, rapturous death imaginable.
She dies, too, as if to pay a debt
  • to her humanity
  • for she had been born into the human condition
  • as all mortals must.

Then the Father with paternal pride
  • reunites body and soul
  • of the Virgin Mother of his Son.
And she is waft to paradise.

The Fifth Glorious Mystery

Why the Coronation of Mary?

A Royal Flush

Reverie: Our reverie continues as we peek into eternity.
Another celestial celebration awaits.
Another extraordinary reunion,
· this time mother and Son are reunited.

How the heavenly hosts must have
· watched with wonder and awe as
· Jesus in his glorified body
· meets, welcomes, embraces ardently
· Mother Mary in her glorified body.

Mother and Son together again,
· never more to suffer,
· never more to die,
· never.

Then, as the Father once crowned the Son
· the Son now crowns the mother.
Prior to his ascension, Jesus declared:

> "All things have been handed
> over to me by my Father" (Lk 10:22).

The Son now shares his kingship
· with his mother.

He, Jesus, king of heaven and earth.
King of all creation.
She, Mary, queen of heaven and earth.
Queen of the universe.
What a royal family we have in heaven.
And membership into this regal ménage
· is open to all of us
· through baptism, sanctifying grace,
· through our holy lives.

Hence, all those billions upon billions
  • of enslaved, oppressed men, women, children
      down the ages
  • but devout and believing always,
  • now royalty.

Billions upon billions of disenfranchised, despised,
      downtrodden masses
  • but tried and true Christians all their lives,
  • now royalty.

And the middle classes,
  • those who subordinated the material,
  • their property and possessions,
  • to the spiritual:
  • God, soul, salvation,

Now royalty too.
What of the royalty of earth?
They who accepted, acknowledged Jesus as their King
  • and served him with love and loyalty,
  • now laugh at the straw and stubble
  • their thrones, titles, and kingdoms were here below.

For there is but one kingdom,
  • the kingdom of God in heaven,
  • a kingdom of life and love,
  • a kingdom of peace and joy,
  • a kingdom that lasts forevermore.

Wow!

Appendices:
Varia Rosaria

Evolution of the Rosary

Prior to Twelfth Century

- **Prayers Employed:** The 150 psalms from the psalter sung or recited in monasteries are replaced by 150 Our Fathers ("pater nosters") for monks and laity who don't know Latin. This was called "Poor People's Psalter."
- **Meditation Material:** Phrases from psalms are inserted between the Our Fathers for meditation purposes.
- **Physical Form:** Fingers, sticks, stones, pebbles.

Around the Twelfth or Thirteenth Centuries

- **Prayers Employed:** The 150 Our Fathers are replaced by 150 Hail Marys when devotions to Jesus and Mary become popular. The 150 Hail Marys are divided into three groups of fifty called "Mary's Chaplets" (Mary's cap or crown).
- **Meditation Material:** Liturgical phrases from feasts of Jesus and Mary are substituted for phrases from the psalter as points for contemplation.
- **Physical Form:** Knotted cords or strings of wooden beads.

Circa Fourteenth and Fifteenth Centuries

- **Prayers Employed:** Feast of Mary's Visitation to Elizabeth prompts "Blessed is the fruit of your womb" to be added to first portion of the Hail Mary prayer. The three chaplets of fifty Hail Marys, are each styled "Rosarium" (Mary's rose garden).
- **Meditation Material:** The three chaplets of fifty Hail Marys each are reduced to fifteen Hail Marys each. The three sets of fifteen Hail Marys are now styled the Joyful, Sorrowful, and Glorious Mysteries with reflections matching the contents of each mystery as today.
- **Physical Form:** Glass beads. Gold and silver chains with precious stones for beads become fashionable with the wealthy.

By about the Early Fifteenth Century

- **Prayers Employed:** The 150 Hail Marys are divided into groups of ten, called "decades," with Our Fathers interspersed. These rosary prayers now become popular, even as daily prayers, among the populace.
- **Meditation Material:** Meditation is now confined to ten Hail Marys preceded by one Our Father and a Glory Be.
- **Physical Form:** Knotted cords by the poor. Strings of beads by general population. Gold, silver chains by the rich. This remains unchanged to the present.

During the Fifteenth Century

- **Prayers Employed:** Same as above.
- **Meditation Material:** The Fifth Glorious Mystery (Coronation of Mary) is conjoined to Fourth Glorious Mystery (Assumption of Mary). The Fifth Glorious Mystery now "The Last Judgment," but later this is dropped for the earlier arrangement.

By the Sixteenth Century and Onward

- **Prayers Employed:** The Glory Be is added as a concluding prayer to each decade. The Hail Mary acquires what is now its second part: "Holy Mary Mother of God pray for us sinners … "
- **Meditation Material:** Written cards and "rosary pictures" are attempted— forerunners of modern movies and videotapes on rosary mysteries. Meditation is assigned to beginning or end of each decade.

By the Nineteenth Century

- **Prayers Employed:** Apostles' Creed and one Our Father and three Hail Marys form introduction to the entire rosary.
- **Meditation Material:** No meditation required.

Twentieth Century to Present

- **Prayers Employed:** After the apparitions of Mary at Fatima in 1917, the prayer by Our Lady to the three children is added after the Glory

Be. Religious orders tend to add one more short prayer after the Fatima prayer. "St. Brigit Rosary," also called "Briggitine Rosary," appears with sixty-three beads plus the usual introductory creed, etc., as its pendant. The sixty-three beads represent the supposed sixty-three years of Mary's earthly life.

- **Meditation Material:** Same as before. However, at frequent wakes, before meetings, at gatherings, etc., often only the mystery is announced by leader—or a relevant virtue suggested before each decade with no further points or details added. Daily recitations, especially by busy devotees, are devoid of form meditation.
- **Physical Form:** Traditional wood and glass beads on cords or chains worn around the waist by some religious.

Mid-twentieth Century to Present

- **Prayers Employed:** The pendant of the Briggitine Rosary, on which the crucifix hangs, is adopted and attached to the standard circlet of beads throughout the world. Also a mini-rosary for economy of space is introduced, consisting of a pendant and only one decade representing all fifteen to be repeated as needed.
- **Meditation Material:** Meditation on Mary's joys, sorrows, and triumphs.
- **Physical Form:** Plastic cross and plastic beads on cords for children and poorer people is added to rosary arsenal.

Twenty-first Century

On October 16, 2002, the Feast of Our Lady of the Rosary, Pope John Paul II issues his apostolic letter *Rosarium Virginis Mariae*, in which he introduces Five Mysteries of Light to fill the void between the traditional Joyful and Sorrowful Mysteries and declares the Year of the Rosary: October 2002 to October 2003.

Some Rosary Greats

In General

First and foremost
    Jesus, Mary, Joseph,
    principals in the rosarian mysteries.

Then St. Dominic (1170–1221)
    who is popularly presented
    as receiving the rosary from Mary
    to be handed down to his followers
    and passed on to all peoples
    in their own languages, thus
    helping them to understand the mysteries of the Mass
    still offered in Latin.

In Particular

1. Alan deRupe (1425–1475), Dominican friar
    whose "Confraternity of the Rosary"
    gave the devotion great impetus
    from 1470 on under its first name,
    the "Psalter of Jesus and Mary."

2. Pope Pius V—a Dominican
    who had the confraternity members
    praying in the streets of Rome
    on Sunday, October 7, 1571,
    as the Battle of Lepanto raged
    between the Christian fleet and that of Islam
    for the survival of Christianity in Europe,
    resulting in a decisive Christian victory
    and the subsequent Feast of the Most Holy Rosary
    proclaimed by the jubilant pontiff.

3. Pope Clement XI— who decreed in 1716
   the Feast of the Most Holy Rosary
   be universally celebrated every October 7.

4. St. Louis Marie de Montefort (1673–1716)
   who wrote a remarkable book
   entitled *The Wonderful Secrets of the Most
      Holy Rosary*,
   which profoundly influenced and enhanced
   the spiritual growth of Christians everywhere
   for many generations to come.

5. St. Bernadette (1844–1879)
   who recited the rosary at the grotto
   as Mary held a shiny one in her hand,
   resulting in millions of rosary beads to be
   in motion at Lourdes to this day.

6. The three children at Fatima in 1917
   of whom two are now beatified,
   were requested by Mary
   in her apparition to them
   to recite the rosary daily
   for peace in the world.

7. St. Juan Diego (canonized August 1, 2002),
   the only saint to be shown
   a picture of the Blessed Virgin,
   now known as Our Lady of Guadalupe,
   and this, on the saint's grass cloak,
   thus prompting thousands of pilgrims
   arriving and departing the Mexican shrine,
   especially the Native Americans and Mestizos,
   to pray the rosary and sing hymns in Mary's honor.

Rosarian Liturgies

Joyful Mysteries

Annunciation	March 25
Visitation	May 31
Nativity	December 25
Presentation	February 2

Sorrowful Mysteries

Crucifixion	Good Friday

Glorious Mysteries

Resurrection	Easter Sunday
Ascension	Fortieth Day after Easter
Descent of the Holy Spirit	Pentecost Sunday
Assumption of Mary	August 15
Coronation (Queenship of Mary)	August 22
Our Lady of the Rosary	October 7